Five-Minute Bible and Fun

by
Shery Koons Borenstein

illustrated by Veronica Terrill

Cover by Jeff Van Kanegan

Shining Star Publications, Copyright © 1992

A Division of Frank Schaffer Publications, Inc.

ISBN No. 0-86653-698-1

Printing No. 98

Shining Star Publications
23740 Hawthorne Blvd.
Torrance, CA 90505

Unless otherwise indicated, the New International Version of the Bible was used in preparing the activities in this book.

Dedication

To my newest student,
Sarah Elizabeth Borenstein,
God's gift for instructing me
in the time-honored teaching profession
of motherhood.

Special Appreciation

To Pastor and Mrs. Jim Conley
for their spiritual guidance and instruction,
and for the time they took reviewing the manuscript for this book.

To Miss Megan Goldstrom
for joyfully working out many of these exercises.
To my husband, Jim, for his encouragement, love, and assistance
as I spent many long, creative hours doing a task I truly enjoyed.

Of course, I must thank Becky Daniel of Shining Star Publications
for giving me the privilege of ministering to a large classroom of children
through this book and other publications.

SS2828

Introduction

Five-Minute Bible Games and Fun has been designed with both the teacher and the student in mind. So often, busy teachers wish for brief, yet worthwhile, activities for aiding them in their teaching. They desire assistance with those few moments before class "officially" begins, or they long for help in making a smooth and beneficial transition from one activity to another. Perhaps, too, they face the dilemma of several "leftover" minutes before the parent arrives and class is dismissed. For nearly all substitute teachers there is the nagging possibility of just not having enough material to teach. This book is for those teachers! It has been prepared with plenty of profitable exercises that can be applied to nearly any teaching situation. Minimal preparation on the part of the teacher is necessary.

For students, *Five-Minute Bible Games and Fun* is not only fun, but it is also worthy of their time. Each page is created with Bible-based character training in mind. The activities are also intended to be both brief and enjoyable learning adventures for every student.

Although this book was designed with a "classroom setting" in mind, *Five-Minute Bible Games and Fun* can also be a tremendous addition to a family's devotional time. Whether you have one child or several, these activities fit in handily for special Bible-enriched learning experiences.

Keep several pages handy to be used by your students. They are sure to be a class-time highlight for everyone!

Table of Contents

Recipe for Making Friends

Use the ingredients listed here, or create some of your own, to fill in the "Friendship Recipe" below.

Ingredients:

kindness	laughter
forgiveness	sharing
love	prayers
time	honesty
togetherness	

Friendship Recipe

Sift together 2 cups of _____ and $1\frac{1}{2}$

tablespoons of _____. Stir in 3 cups of

_____. Combine _____ with

the above ingredients. Add _____ and mix

thoroughly. Sprinkle on _____.

Use this recipe often to provide good and lasting friendships!

SS2828

Friendship Clue

Discover the path that reveals a clue for making friends. If you take the correct path, you will read a Bible sentence about friendship. Starting at the word *you*, follow the proper path. Write down each letter as you follow it. Do not cross a solid line.

____ ____ ____ ____   ____ ____ ____

____ ____ ____ ____ ____   ____ ____ ____   ____ ____

____ ____ ____ ____   ____ ____ ____ ____

Proverbs 18:24 KJV

SS2828

A Friendly Message

Following the color code,
Color in the grid below.
You will find a message there,
Telling you how much friends care!

Color Code

∴ = pink
〰 = yellow or gold
• = red
✕ = light green

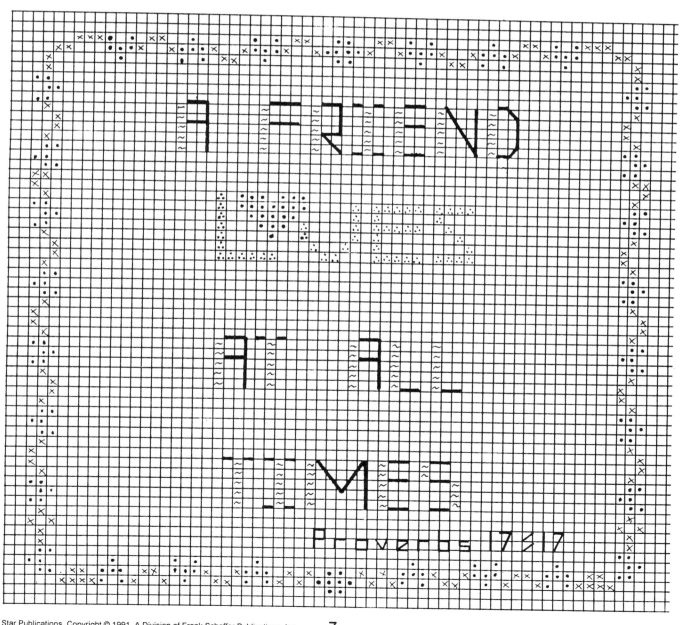

Godly Friendships

Read the clues and fill in the puzzle with the names listed here. These are all Bible people who were good friends.

Abraham   Christy

Daniel

Jonathan   Naomi   Paul

Bible Clues

1. He was known as a friend of sinners. (Matthew 11:19)

2. The Bible calls this man "God's friend." (James 2:23)

3. Hananiah, Mishael, and Azariah were friends of this brave young man. (Daniel 1:11-12)

4. David was a special friend of this young man who was the son of the king. (1 Samuel 18:3)

5. This mother-in-law had a very special friend in her daughter-in-law Ruth. (Ruth 1:15-16)

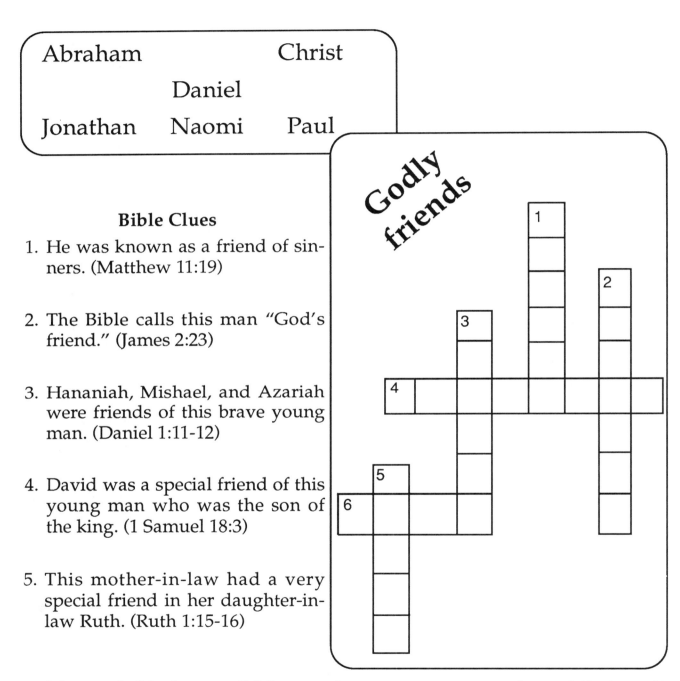

6. Silas and this famous Bible preacher sang songs together while in jail! (Acts 16:25)

Keys to Being Friendly

Color the keys that tell kind ways of being friendly. Cross out (X) the keys that describe ways that are not friendly.

"But a Samaritan, as he traveled, . . . bandaged his wounds, . . . and took care of him."

Luke 10:33-34

"Be kind and compassionate to one another, forgiving each other, just as in Christ God forgave you."

Ephesians 4:32

Choosing Friends

God wants His children to choose the right kind of friends. Decode the Scripture verse below to see what kind of friends a Christian should choose.

"___ ___ m ___ fr ___ ___ n d t ___

___ l l w h ___ f ___ ___ r y ___ ___ ,

t ___ ___ l l w h ___ f ___ l l ___ w

y ___ ___ r p r ___ c ___ p t s." Psalm 119:63

The Best Friend

"... I have called you friends. ..."

John 15:15

The letters from the verse phrase above are mixed up in the box below. Beginning with the first letter–I, find each letter of the verse and cross it out. There will be five letters left over. Write down the five remaining letters on the lines at the bottom of the page. Then, unscramble the letters to find the name of the One who wants to be your very best friend.

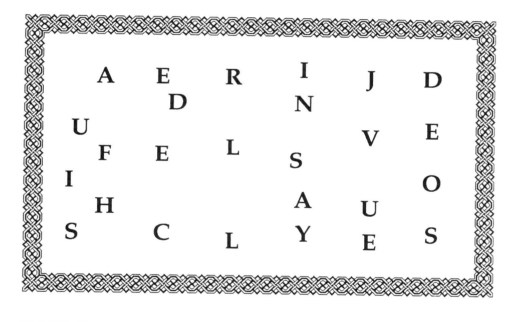

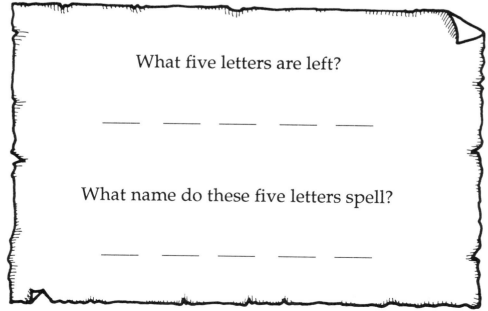

What five letters are left?

____ ____ ____ ____ ____

What name do these five letters spell?

____ ____ ____ ____ ____

SS2828

Friendship Certificate

"But the fruit of the spirit is love, joy, peace, patience, kindness, goodness, faithfulness, gentleness and self-control. Against such things there is no law." Galatians 5:22-23

Fill in and color the Friendship Certificate below. Then cut it out and give it to one of your special friends.

Certificate of Friendship

This certificate is being awarded to my friend

_____
(Place the name of a friend here.)

for showing excellence in

_____,
(List something special about your friend.)

given on this day, _____.
(Write in today's date.)

Thanks for being my friend!

_____
(Sign your name here.)

SS2828

Friendly Fuzzies

People sometimes refer to receiving nice words or rewards as getting a "warm fuzzy." They like to hear nice things said to them. Even your friends appreciate hearing kind words from you. On the fuzzy animals pictured here, write down some nice things you can say to your friends. Color the shapes, and, if you wish, you can even cut them out to give to your friends!

Ode to Friends

Following the sample unrhymed poem, write your own poem about friends. Use your own ideas or choose from the list of words below.

Friends–
Caring, loving, giving
Ready to listen
Funny, enjoyable, nice
My buddies!

Friends–

_____, _____, _____

(List three action words–verbs, ending in "ing.")

People I like to be with–

_____, _____, _____

(List three describing words–adjectives.)

My special playmates!

Action words–"ing" verbs		Describing words–adjectives	
loving	playing	kind	genuine
sharing	entertaining	sweet	real
smiling	encouraging	fun	loyal
laughing	willing	best	good
hugging	understanding	special	helpful
forgiving	supporting	joyful	active
		delightful	patient

SS2828

Take the Initiative!

"Honor your father and your mother. . . ."

Exodus 20:12

Connect the dots beginning at letter A. You will discover a picture relating to a household task you can do without being asked. If you wish, you may color the picture.

I Can Do This!

Look at the pictures on this page. Do you see any tasks that you can do? Circle the ones you can do. Try to do some of these this week without being asked!

What Is Initiative?

"... When he was in the house, he asked them, 'What were you arguing about ...?'" Mark 9:33

Fill in the shapes that have this sign • in them. You will discover the special meaning of the big word initiative.

SS2828

Who Can Help?

"May your hand be ready to help me. . . ."   Psalm 119:173

If you are a boy, color the boy shape with the same color of hair and eyes that you have. If you are a girl, color the girl shape with the same color of hair and eyes that you have. Write your name in the box on the paper figure. Cut out the shape and place it in your bedroom as a reminder that you can help with many things.

18   SS2828

Homemade Help

Unscramble the words in each soap bubble. These are names of things that you can help with around the house.

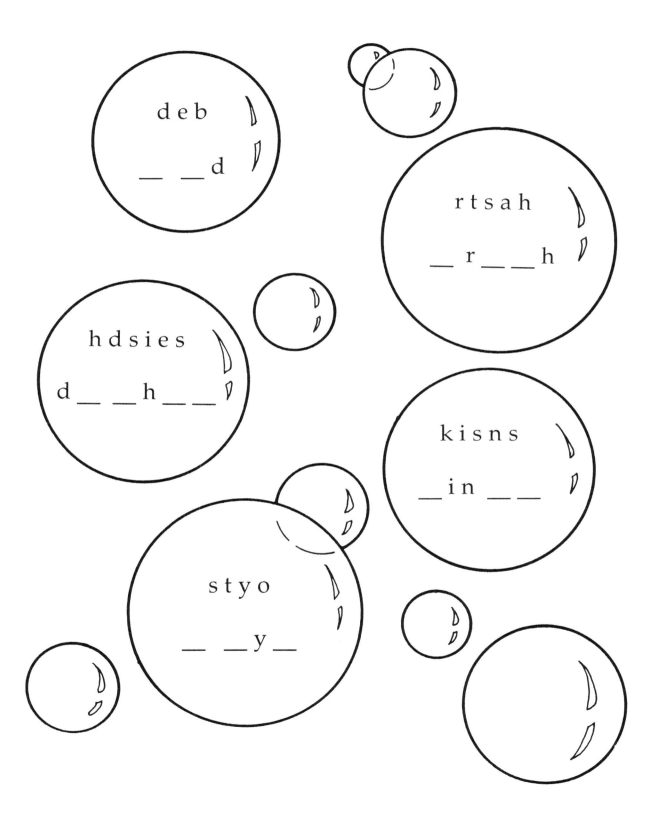

d e b

_ _ d

r t s a h

_ r _ _ h

h d s i e s

d _ _ h _ _

k i s n s

_ i n _ _

s t y o

_ _ y _

SS2828

Spell J-O-Y

"He will be a joy and delight to you, and many will rejoice because of his birth,"   Luke 1:14

Would you like to know the best way to have joy? Decode the puzzle below to find out how.
First go through the boxes and write down every letter that has a number 1 assigned to it.
Do the same for the letters that have a number 2 and a number 3.

1	2	3	1	2	3	3	1
J	O	Y	E	T	O	U	S
2	3	1	3	2	3	1	2
H	R	U	S	E	E	S	R
	2	3	3				
	S	L	F				

__ __ __ __ __ is first.

__ __ __ __ __ __ are second.

__ __ __ __ __ __ __ __ comes last.

SS2828

Joyful Fruit

"But the fruit of the Spirit is . . . joy . . . ."   Galatians 5:22

When you know the Lord Jesus as your Savior, you have a constant source of joy. There are things that you can do to help your joy in Christ become more fruitful. On four of the grapes below, write several things that you do or could do to make your joy more fruitful. (Several ideas are already written to help you.)

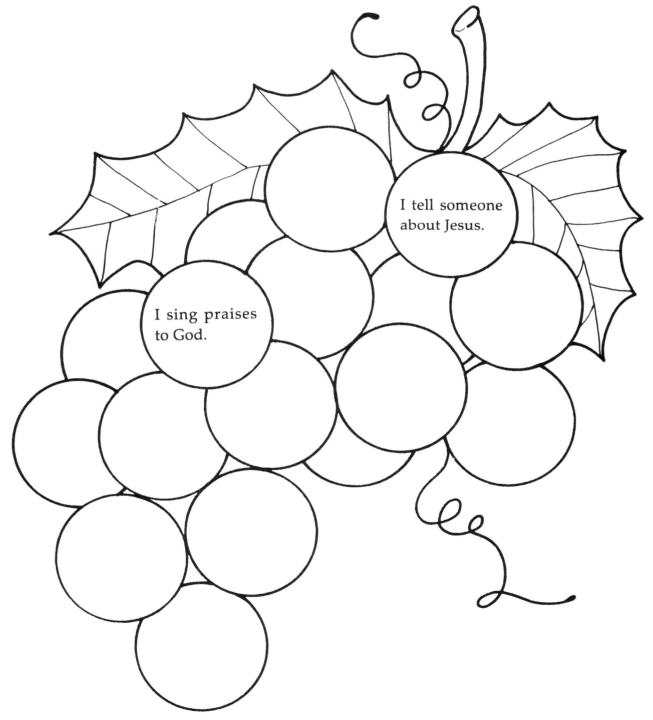

Joyful Phrases

How many joyful phrases do you know? Try to see how many of these Bible quotations you can match. Read the phrase on each balloon. Match the first part of the verse with the part that follows. To show that you know both parts of the verse, color those balloons the same color. For example, these balloons would be colored the same:

"... rejoicing comes in the

morning."
Psalm 30:5

"Restore to me

"Those who sow in tears

in heaven over one sinner who repents. ..."
Luke 15:7

take away your joy."
John 16:22

"... there will be more rejoicing

they were overjoyed."
Matthew 2:10

"But the fruit of the Spirit

"... and no one will

the joy of your salvation. ..."
Psalm 51:12

will reap with songs of joy."
Psalm 126:5

"When they saw the star,

is love, joy. ..."
Galatians 5:22

Joy-Filled Duty

Who do you think is the best example of a joy-filled person? If you think it is Jesus Christ, you are right! Decode the Bible phrase from Hebrews 12:2b to find out what difficult task Christ joyfully accepted.

 w+ -s-e 4-u   then-n

" _____   _____   _____

 -uice+oy    s+ -n    +4

_____   _____   _____

 -ouse+im   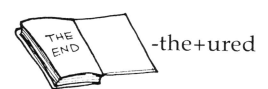 -the+ured

_____   _____

3-re

_____   _____ ."

What difficult task did Christ do for all people?

d___ ed on the ___ r ___ ___ s

Song of Joy

"He put a new song in my mouth. . . ."

Psalm 40:3

When you accepted Christ as your Savior, the Bible says that God put a new song in your mouth (Psalm 40:3). It is a special hymn of praise that will point people to your Savior. It is a true song of joy!

How would you like to write your own song? Using the words from the word list, fill in the blanks below to complete this song. The song can be sung to the tune of "Are You Sleeping, Brother John?"

Word List	
heart	Jesus
joy	passing

Joy in Jesus

Joy in Je- sus! Joy in _____!

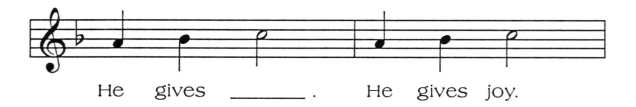

He gives _____. He gives joy.

Joy that's ev- er- last- ing, Joy that's nev-er _____–

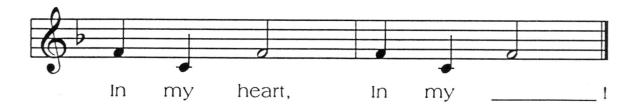

In my heart, In my _____!

Shining Star Publications, Copyright © 1991, A Division of Frank Schaffer Publications, Inc.

SS2828

My Kindness Poster

A Bible verse about kindness:
(Write the verse or phrase about kindness.)

My greatest example for kindness:

(Color the name below.)

JESUS

A song that reminds me to be kind:
(Write the title here.)

"_____"

Some kind people I know:
(Write the names in the box.)

I can be kind to_____
by doing_____
_____.

Some words that show kindness:
(Draw smiling faces by words that show kindness. Draw frowning faces by words that **do not** show kindness.)

forgiving   patient
loving   selfish
mean   friendly

Something I will do this week to show kindness:

(Draw a picture to illustrate what you will do.)

Models of Kindness

Read the clues and unscramble the letters to find the names of Bible people who were kind.

This young man was the son of a king, yet he was generous to David, a shepherd boy.

_ O _ _ T H _ _
ANJTHONA

She showed a tremendous love for Christ by anointing His feet with a costly oil and wiping them with her hair.

_ _ R _
ARMY

When two spies came to her city, this woman showed them kindness by helping them to escape from danger.

R _ _ A _
HARAB

His brothers once sold him as a slave, yet this powerful ruler in Egypt showed great mercy and kindness to them. He gave them food during a time of great famine.

_ _ S _ _ H
OSEPJH

This man patiently and gently helped a poor man who had been robbed, beaten, and left to die.

_ A M _ R _ T _ N
NATIRAMAS

These people were great examples of kindness. They did kind things, not wanting anything in return. Also, they were not seeking men's praise for their deeds.

Shining Star Publications, Copyright © 1991, A Division of Frank Schaffer Publications, Inc.

SS2828

Be Ye Kind

1. Beginning at the circled letter B, circle every other letter until you have gone around the happy face one time.

2. Beginning again at the top letter B, write down the circled letters on the lines below.

3. Next, starting at the starred letter I*, write down the letters not circled until you have gone around the happy face again.

4. Read what you have written. This is a special verse for staying happy.

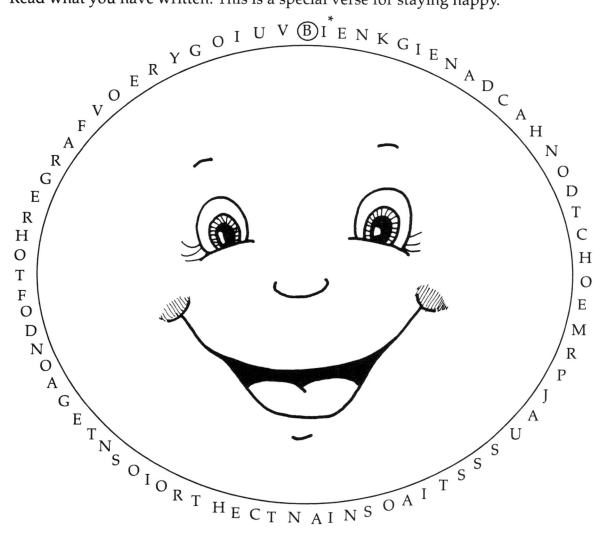

"_ _ _ _ _ _ _ _ _ _ _ _ _ _ _ _ _ _ _ _ _ _ _

_ _ _ _ _ _ _ _ _,' _ _ _ _ _ _ _ _ _ _ _ _ _ _ _ _ _

_ _ _ _ _, _ _ _ _ _ _ _ _ _ _ _ _ _ _

_ _ _ _ _ _ _ _ _ _ _ _ _ _." (Ephesians 4:32)

SS2828

Kindness "Kwiz"

"and to godliness, brotherly kindness; and to brotherly kindness, love."   2 Peter 1:7

Place a check mark in the box that best describes the way you act in the given situations. Then follow the instructions below to discover your "kindness" score.

_____ 1. When given the opportunity to open a door for another person, I

☐ always ☐ sometimes ☐ never open a door for that person.

_____ 2. If I have a new toy when friends come to visit, I

☐ always ☐ sometimes ☐ never let them play with it.

_____ 3. I ☐ always ☐ sometimes ☐ never go out of my way to make a visitor feel welcome in my house or my classroom.

_____ 4. In talking to my family members, I ☐ always ☐ sometimes

☐ never treat them with special love and respect.

_____ 5. If there is something I have that I could give to someone in need, I

☐ always ☐ sometimes ☐ never give it to that person.

_____ **Total Score**

Scoring for the "Kwiz":

Put a +5 (plus five) on the line beside the sentence where you have checked the word *always*.

Write a +2 (plus two) on the line beside the sentence where you have checked the word *sometimes*.

Place a -2 (minus two) on the line beside the sentence where you have checked the word *never*.

If your score is +20 to +25, you are a classy, charitable chum. Keep up the good work!

If your score is +10 to +19, you are a comfortably kind kid. Work a little harder!

If your score is -10 to +9, you are a casually concerned child. Beginning now, try to be kinder!

SS2828

Lighten the Load

Color the picture with bright colors. Write one kind word on each kite pictured below. Try to use these words when talking to others today. Your kind words may help to lighten their loads!

          SS2828

Which Kind?

Read the sentences below. Decide if the deed is kind or unkind. If the deed is kind, then color the smiling face. If it is unkind, color the frowning face.

	Kind	Unkind

You see your mom carrying in the groceries, but you don't offer to help. Are you being kind or unkind?

Your dad comes home tired after a long day at work. You offer to hang up his coat and put away his things. Are you being kind or unkind?

Your sweet, elderly neighbor is doing some yard work. You offer to help her. Are you being kind or unkind?

Your little brother fell and skinned his knee. You call him a "baby" and tell him, "Get up and stop crying!" Are you being kind or unkind?

Your friend tells you that she has a report to give at school. She is afraid and nervous. You tell her that you will pray for her to do a good job. Are you being kind or unkind?

Shining Star Publications, Copyright © 1991, A Division of Frank Schaffer Publications, Inc.

SS2828

Acts of Kindness

"in purity, understanding, patience and kindness. . . ."   2 Corinthians 6:6

Even simple acts of kindness are pleasing to God when they are done out of a loving heart. On each hand shape below, write the name of someone you will help this week. Below the name, describe a way you can show kindness to that person. (A sample has been given to help you.)

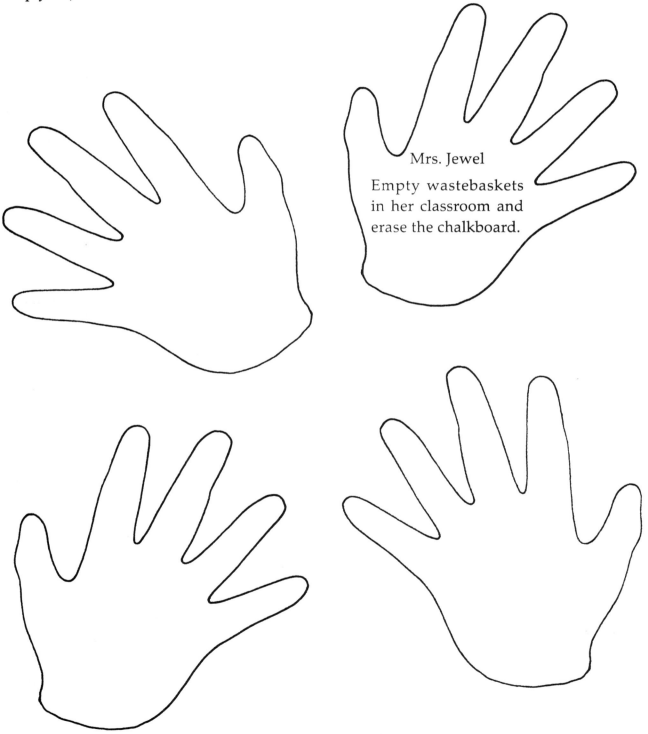

Mrs. Jewel
Empty wastebaskets in her classroom and erase the chalkboard.

Live in Kindness

Fill in the missing words to this poem by using rhyming words found in the circle below.

asked
way
week
you

In everything you do and say,

You should do it in a very kind _____.

"Please" and "thank you" are words to speak–

Not just sometime, but throughout the _____.

Helping others without being _____

Is the best way to show a kind act.

So be kind in all you do.

Then you will see God working through _____ !

Kindness Reminder

Color the bookmark below and cut it out. Punch a hole where the circle is and put string or ribbon through the hole. Use this bookmark as a reminder to be kind to others.

"LOVE is patient, LOVE is kind."

1 Corinthians 13:4a

SS2828

A Command to Love

Read the message below to see what commandment God has given to His children. Next, see how many words from the verse you can find in the puzzle. Use only words going down or across. Circle the words as you find them in the heart shape.

"... Love one another.
As I have loved you. ..."
John 13:34

F	K	L	A	S	P	J	R
R	T	O	N	E	Y	O	U
G	C	V	O	I	S	H	T
J	V	E	T	1	3	N	Z
L	3	4	H	A	V	E	U
L	O	V	E	D	A	K	Q
X	B	Q	R	W	G	U	N

SS2828

Loving God

Think of boys and girls that love God. Look at the descriptions below. Put a smiley face beside the things that Christian children do to show their love for God. Put a frowning face beside the things that Christian children may do that don't show love for God.

Memorizing Bible verses

Disobeying parents

Attending church

Talking to God in prayer

Reading the Bible

Lying to others

Fighting with brothers and sisters

Telling others about God's love

Helping the needy

Singing songs of praise

Looking at wicked things

Being selfish

SS2828

God's Gift of Love

"Yet to all who *received* him, to those who *believed* in his *name*, he *gave* the *right* to become *children* of *God*–"

John 1:12

God gave you the very best gift ever when He gave His Son, Jesus, to die for you. When you receive Him as your Savior, you become part of God's family.

Fill in the blanks with the words on the gifts below to find a special promise from John 1:12.

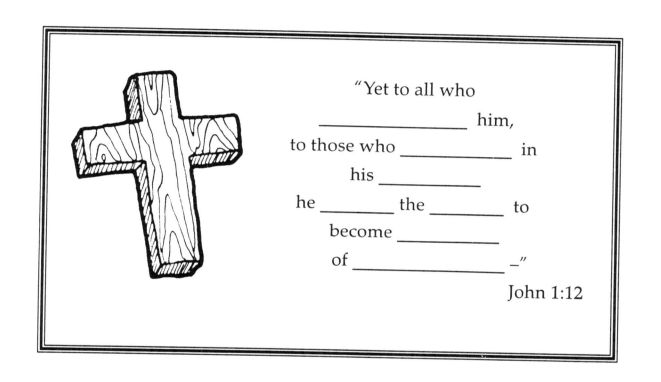

Adopted!

God truly has a special way of showing His love for you—by adopting you as His child. Have you ever been adopted into His family? If you have trusted Christ as your Savior, then you are His adopted child.

Fill in the blanks on this Certificate of Adoption. Then color the certificate to make it especially attractive. If you wish, you can place it in your Bible as a reminder of your adoption!

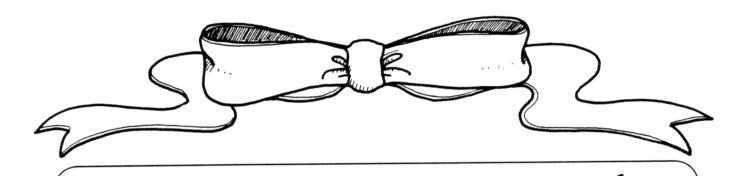

Certificate of Adoption

I, _____, am a child of the King of
   (Write your name here.) Heaven.

My adoption took place

_____.

(Write in the date you were saved. If you don't know the actual date, then write in the age you were or where you were when you accepted Christ as your Savior.)

I know that I have been adopted, because God's Word
tells me so in _____.

(Write in the reference for a Bible verse about salvation.)

       SS2828

Source of Love

Cut out the puzzle shapes below. Piece them together to find out the message written on the puzzle. The message tells you where true love comes from. 1 John 4:8

SS2828

Everlasting Love

In Romans 8:38-39 we are told of things that cannot separate us from God's love. These things are listed below. Write down the letters that are in the boxes; then arrange them to complete the message at the bottom of the page.

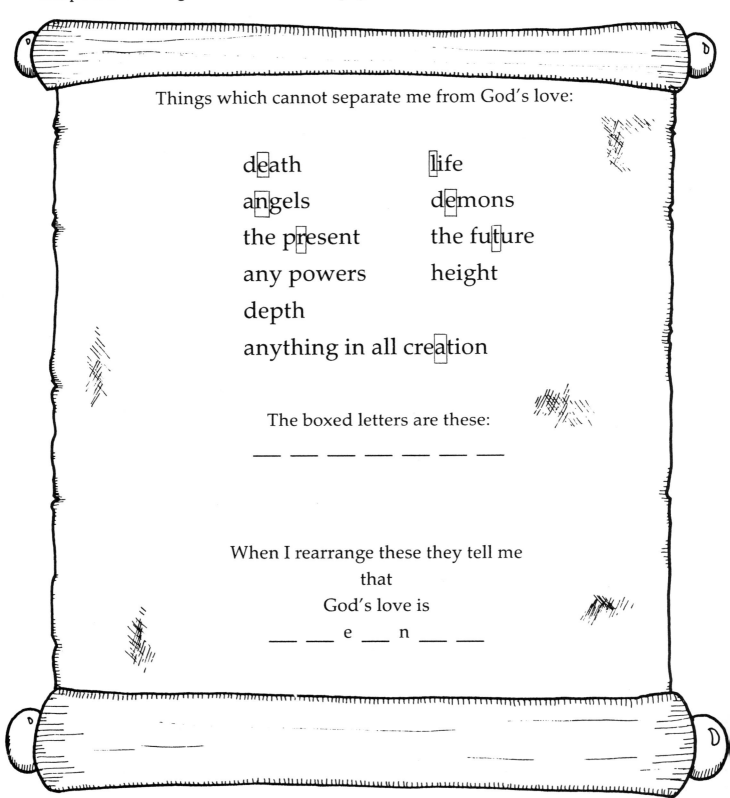

Things which cannot separate me from God's love:

death   life

angels   demons

the present   the future

any powers   height

depth

anything in all creation

The boxed letters are these:

— — — — — — —

When I rearrange these they tell me
that
God's love is
— — e — n — —

SS2828

Family Love

On each heart shape below, write the name of a family member (it can be a grandparent or other relative, too). Then write an idea or draw a picture in that heart of something you can do for that person. It may be a simple task, like picking up your toys or reading a story to a younger brother. Try to do this task in the coming week. Do it without making a big show of yourself and with a true heart of love.

Living in "Harmony House"

This is a read-along-story. As your teacher or another student reads this story, follow along. Use the picture code to help you with the story. After you have heard the story, color the pictures of the houses and fill in the answers at the end of the page.

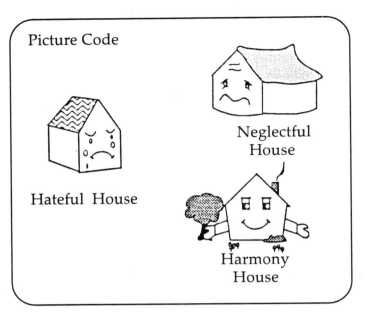

If houses could speak, they would have many stories to tell. These houses , and  have their own stories to tell.

 on Forsaken Road is a house filled with anger. The people who live in  often yell and fight bitterly with one another. They rarely ever show any kindness or speak sweetly to each other. If  could speak, he would wipe his tear-filled eyes and plead, "Please stop fighting, Mom, Dad, and children, and heed what James 1:19-20 says: "Everyone should be quick to listen, slow to speak and slow to become angry, for man's anger does not bring about the righteous life that God desires."

Just around the corner on Thoughtless Street you will find . The family living here isn't necessarily angry or mean. They just don't seem to pay much attention to one another. All members of this family are so-o-o busy with their own wants and activities!

This causes them to look at themselves and forget the needs of the other members of their family. The son living here doesn't realize how much he needs his dad to spend time with him, and the overly occupied dad isn't aware of how much his son needs his care and attention. , if he could speak, would graciously request, "Please stop being so selfish. Instead, obey God's command to '. . . look not only to your own interests, but also to the interests of others.' (Philippians 2:4) Then you will discover how much you really need each other."

Down on Charity Land is not just another house. is a home filled with joyful laughter, music, words of praise, and precious moments of prayer. It is the kind of home that anyone can have, although it takes work. is a home where the forgiving love of Jesus Christ has been placed. The dad, mom and children have accepted the free gift of God's salvation. Although they are not perfect, each has given his/her life to God's will and control. If could speak, he would smile broadly and say, "Thank you for showing God's love through the lives you live in our home. Because of you, many will see God and will desire to know Him."

In which house do you live , , or ? Are you doing your part to make your home a ?

* * * * * * * * *

Here are some things I plan to do to make my home happier:

1. _____

2. _____

3. _____

What's in a Name?

Did you know that God knows you by name? Think of that! The God who made the universe, who holds the world together and controls all things, still takes the time to know each one of us by name. What a loving God we have! Here is a special name certificate for you to fill in and color. Use it as a reminder that God knows and loves you.

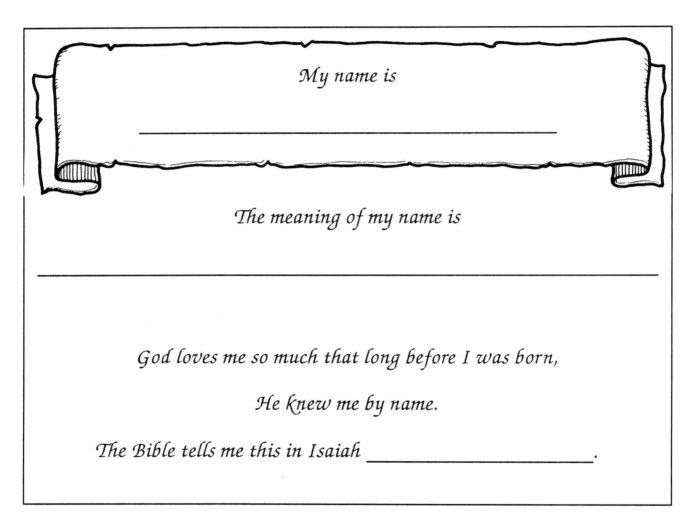

My name is

_____

The meaning of my name is

_____

God loves me so much that long before I was born,

He knew me by name.

The Bible tells me this in Isaiah _____.

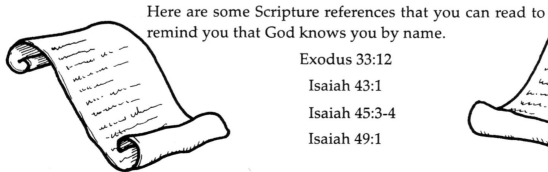

Here are some Scripture references that you can read to remind you that God knows you by name.

Exodus 33:12

Isaiah 43:1

Isaiah 45:3-4

Isaiah 49:1

Obey in Little Things

"Children, obey your parents in everything, for this pleases the Lord."   Colossians 3:20

Do your parents ever ask you to help set the table? How quickly do you obey them? Practice setting the table below. Cut out the plate, drinking glass, napkin, and silverware. Next, glue them on the table in the proper places.

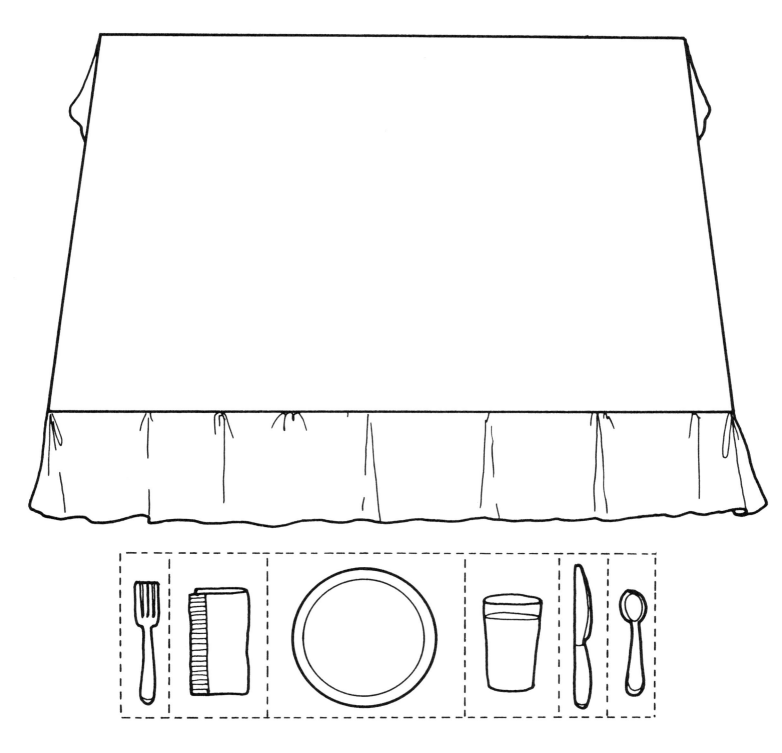

Obedient or Disobedient?

Circle ⬭ the pictures of the Bible people who obeyed God's instructions to them. Cross out ✗ the pictures of those who disobeyed God's directions.

Eve

Cain

Noah

Abraham

Israelites

Jonah

Esther

Christ

Obedience Trail

Follow the obedience trail below. Read each Bible passage. Fill in the blanks telling whom or what you are to obey. (Several letters have been given to help you.)

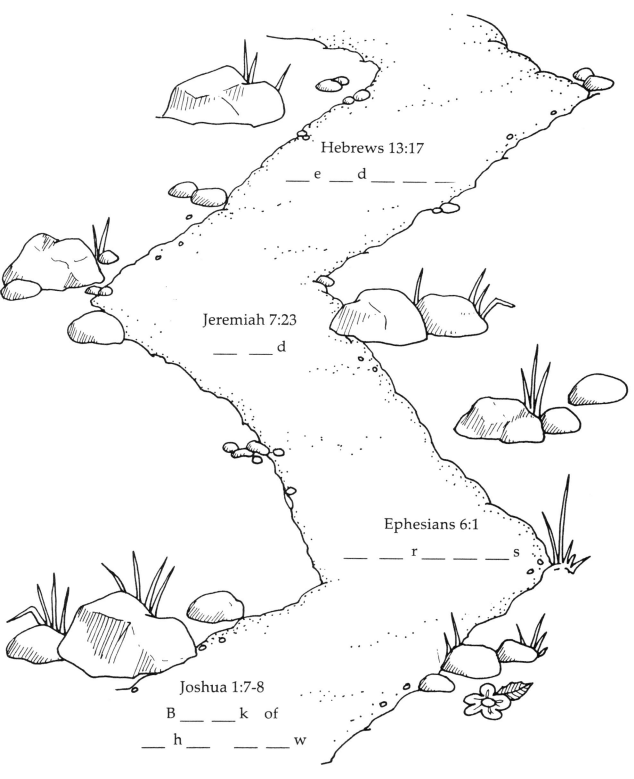

Hebrews 13:17

__ e __ d __ __ __ __ __

Jeremiah 7:23

__ __ __ d

Ephesians 6:1

__ __ __ r __ __ __ __ s

Joshua 1:7-8

B __ __ __ k of

__ h __ __ __ __ w

SS2828

Obedience Displayed

Complete the picture by connecting the dots starting at number 1 and ending at number 10. See how Christ is the greatest example of obedience. Read the Scripture at the bottom of the page.

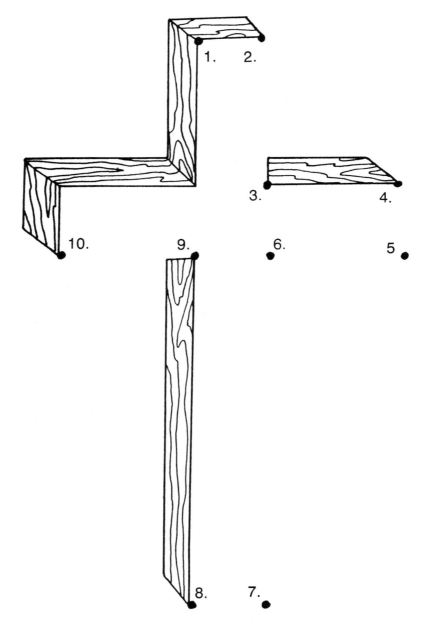

"Your attitude should be the same as that of Christ Jesus: Who, being in very nature God, . . . humbled himself and became obedient to death–even death on a cross!"
Philippians 2:5-8

SS2828

Words of Peace

People who love God's Word are people who have peace in their hearts. Cut out the puzzle pieces below; then put them together to read the words of Psalm 119:165.

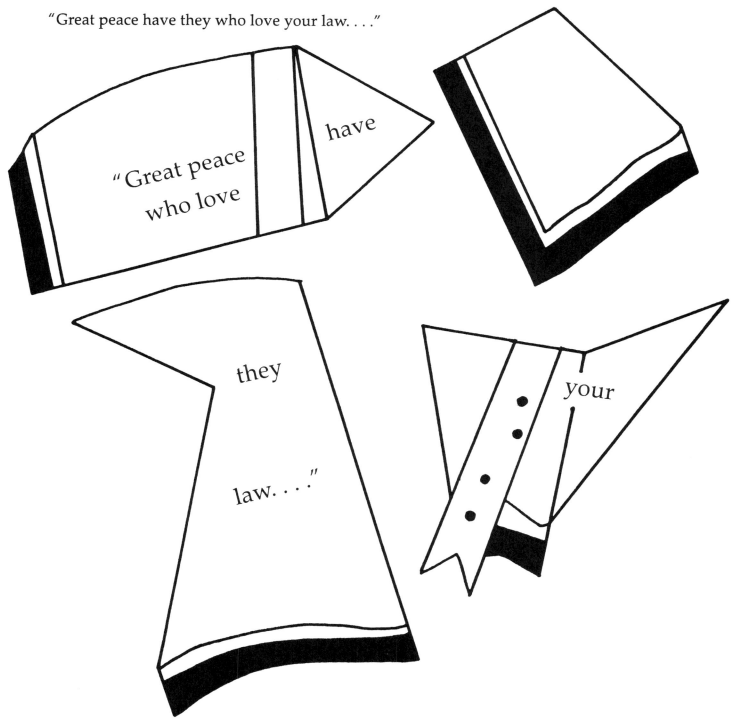

"Great peace have they who love your law. . . ."

SS2828

Song of Peace

Color in the grayed notes (♩) for the song below. Then, using the picture code read the words to "Jesus Loves Me." Let the song remind you that Jesus is the true giver of peace. He gives peace by being with you and by preparing a heavenly home for you.

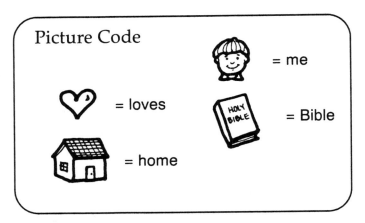

Jesus Loves Me

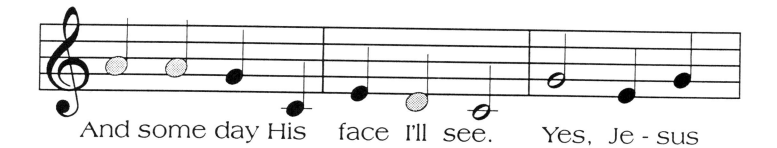

And some day His face I'll see. Yes, Je - sus

! Yes, Je - sus ! Yes, Je - sus

! The tells me so.

Text: Anna B. Warner

Music: William B. Bradbury

SS2828

Restful Peace

"I will lie down and sleep in peace, for you alone, O Lord, make me dwell in safety."

Psalm 4:8

Read the verse above. Color the picture of the sleeping child. Let this be a reminder that God is with you always. You don't need to be afraid.

Beautiful Feet

"How beautiful on the mountains are the feet of those who bring good news, who proclaim peace, who bring good tidings, who proclaim salvation. . . !" Isaiah 52:7

On the foot shape below, write the names of people you know who tell others about Christ.

SS2828

Lasting Peace

Fill in the missing words by looking at the pictures below. Then check your answer by finding the verse in your Bible. The verse is John 14:27.

 - f + ve   ∪

"Peace I _____ with _____; my peace

 - ft + ve   - k

I _____ you.   I do _____

 - ft + ve   🌍

_____ to you as the _____ gives.

 -k

Do _____ let your _____ be troubled. . . ."

God's Creation

We have a powerful God. Think of all the things He has created! In Genesis chapter one and two, we read about the things God made. Looking at the pictures below, see if you can match the things that go together. One has already been matched to help you.

moon

land

man

tree

fruit

water

birds

dark sky with stars

fish

sunny sky with billowy clouds

animals

woman

SS2828

Even the Waves Obey Him!

Based on Luke 8:22-25

Read the story using the picture code to help you.

Picture Code

⛨ = Jesus

👤👤👤 = disciples

🛶 = boat

〰️ = waves

⛈️ = storm

One evening ⛨ and His 👤👤👤 were out in a 🛶 on the sea.

⛨ had been preaching earlier that day. When ⛨ got into the boat,

⛨ decided to rest. While ⛨ was sleeping, a fierce ⛈️ came up.

The 〰️ were strong and broke over the 🛶. The 👤👤👤 became very

fearful! "Wake up, ⛨, for surely we will perish!" the 👤👤👤 cried.

⛨ stood up and said to the wind and the 〰️, "Quiet! Be still." Then

⛨ turned to His 👤👤👤 and said, "Why are you afraid? Do you not

have any faith?"

The 👤👤👤 were amazed. They looked at each other and asked, "Who is this

man? Even the wind and the 〰️ obey ⛨!"

Power of the Gospel

In each box circle the word that doesn't belong. Write it on the matching numbered line below.

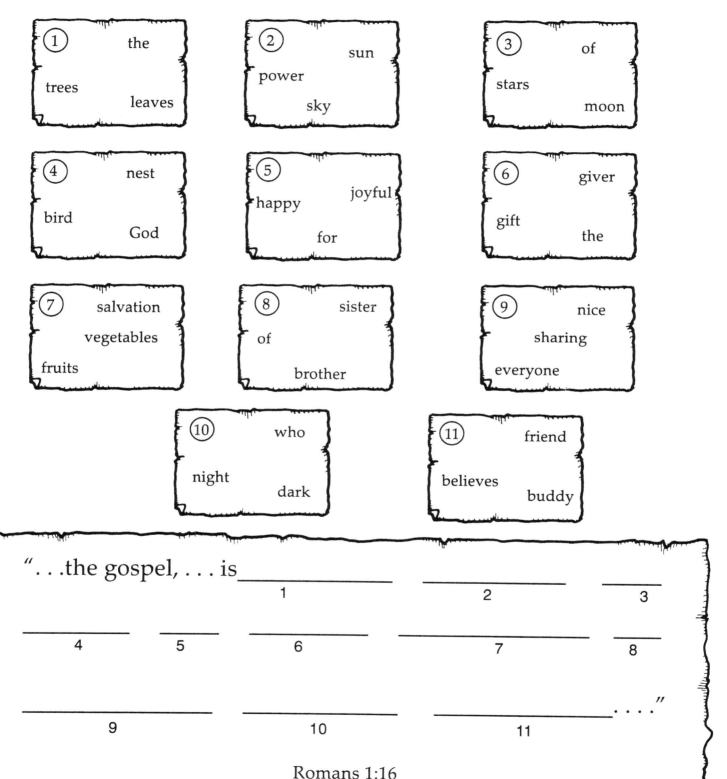

1
the
trees
leaves

2
sun
power
sky

3
of
stars
moon

4
nest
bird
God

5
happy
joyful
for

6
giver
gift
the

7
salvation
vegetables
fruits

8
sister
of
brother

9
nice
sharing
everyone

10
who
night
dark

11
friend
believes
buddy

"...the gospel, ... is _____ _____ _____
                          1   2   3

_____ _____ _____ _____ _____
   4   5   6   7   8

_____ _____ _____ ...."
   9   10   11

Romans 1:16

My God Is Powerful

God's power is shown all around you every day of your life. His power is seen in creation, in salvation, in His protection, and in His provision. Draw a picture to illustrate a time when you experienced God's power in your life. Title your illustration. Try to share it with someone to let that person know about your powerful God.

Title:_____

Sharper than a Sword!

Looking at the pictures below, decode the verse from Hebrews. Answer the question at the bottom of the page.

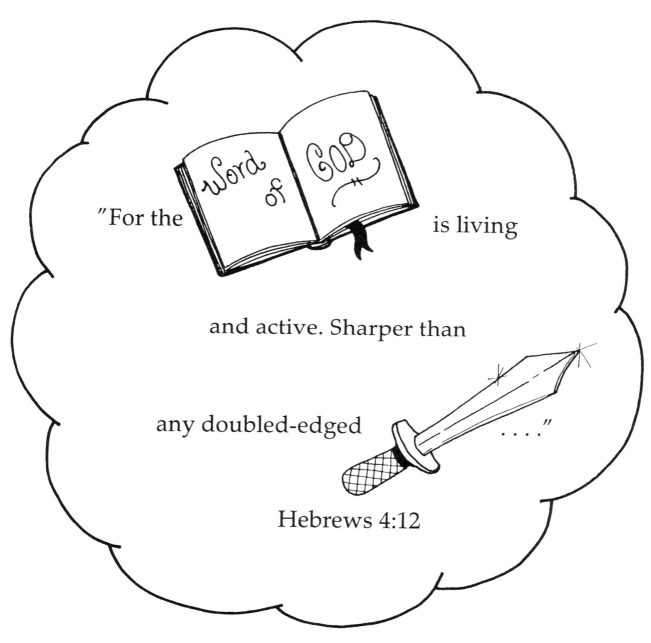

"For the *Word of God* is living

and active. Sharper than

any doubled-edged 🗡 ...."

Hebrews 4:12

According to this verse, what is powerful and sharper than a sword?

W __ __ __   of __ o __

"Food-Full" Prayer

Here is something we are to pray for according to Matthew 6:11. Connect the dots starting at number 1 and finishing at number 15. Then complete the letters by adding one straight line to each letter shape.

Picture a Prayer

"Do not be anxious about anything, but in everything, by prayer and petition, with thanksgiving, present your requests to God."

Philippians 4:6

In Philippians 4:6 we are told not to worry about anything, but we are to pray about everything, and to give thanks for all things. Is there something you are praying for? Draw a picture of something you need. Use it as a reminder to pray and to thank God for His answer.

SS2828

Prayer Poster

Name_____

This is the name of someone who prays for me:

_____

This is the name of someone I pray for:

_____

Fill in the missing words to this Bible example of prayer.

" 'Our Father in _____, hallowed be your name,

your kingdom come,

your will be done on _____ *as it is in* _____.

Give us today our daily _____. *Forgive us our debts,*

as we also have forgiven our debtors. And lead us not into temptation,

but deliver us from the evil one.' " Matthew 6:9-13

SS2828

These are Bible people who prayed:

(Circle the correct names.)

Jesus   Daniel

Tax collector (the publican)

Jonah   Hannah

Moses

Here are some prayer requests for my friends:

Special Requests

Color in the outlined letters for the saying below. You can even cut it out on the dotted lines and use it as a bookmark.

Prayer Stopper

"But the tax collector stood at a distance. He would not even look up to heaven, b breast and said, 'God, have mercy on me, a sinner.' "   Lu

Somewhere hidden in the picture below are three letters. When you find the lette them. Next, unscramble the three letters and write down the word they make. word you find is why God wants you to pray to Him for help in changing your ways.

Why do I need to pray to God for forgiveness?

_____ _____ _____

Praying People

On this page, you will find the names and pictures of various Bible people who prayed. Draw a line from the people's pictures to the descriptions of their prayers. Use your Bible for help.

Daniel

While these men were in jail, they spent their time praying and singing songs.
Acts 16:25

Tax collector
(Publican)

This woman asked God to give her a son. She promised to give him back to God for His use.

1 Samuel 1:10-11

Paul and Silas

This man prayed, "God, have mercy on me, a sinner."

Luke 18:13

Hannah

Even when this man heard the king's message that no one was to pray, he went home and prayed as he always did.

Daniel 6:10

My Prayer

Look at the pictures; then trace the letters for the words found in this prayer.

Dear God,

Thank you for my

family

and my

friends.

Thank you, too, for my

home.

I really want to

thank you for sending

Jesus

to die for my sin.

In Jesus' name, Amen.

SS2828

Family Sharing

"If anyone does not provide for his relatives, and especially for his immediate family, he has denied the faith and is worse than an unbeliever."

I Timothy 5:8

In the boxes below, write down the names of several of your family members (they can also be grandparents). Next, write down or draw pictures of things you have shared with them or they have shared with you.

SS2828

A Message to Share

God has given all His children a special message for them to share. This message is known as the Gospel or the Good News. If you belong to Christ, then you need to share this message, too!

Read the Scripture phrases below and match them with the appropriate pictures. Share this page with someone you know who would like to hear the Good News.

"for all have sinned and fall short of the glory of God,"   Romans 3:23

"For the wages of sin is death. . . ."   Romans 6:23

". . . but the gift of God is eternal life in Christ Jesus our Lord."   Romans 6:23

"This is how we know what love is: Jesus Christ laid down his life for us." 1 John 3:16a

". . . if you confess with your mouth, 'Jesus is Lord,' and believe in your heart that God raised him from the dead, you will be saved."   Romans 10:9

". . . 'Their sins . . . I will remember no more.' "   Hebrews 10:17

Picture Your Sharing

You have the privilege of sharing with people every day. Choose one of the situations listed below. Then draw a picture showing the sharing involved.

1. I shared my time reading a book to a younger child.

2. My friend and I shared our energy by helping Dad with the lawn care.

3. I shared the Gospel message with a new friend.

4. I shared my allowance in Sunday School for a special missionary project.

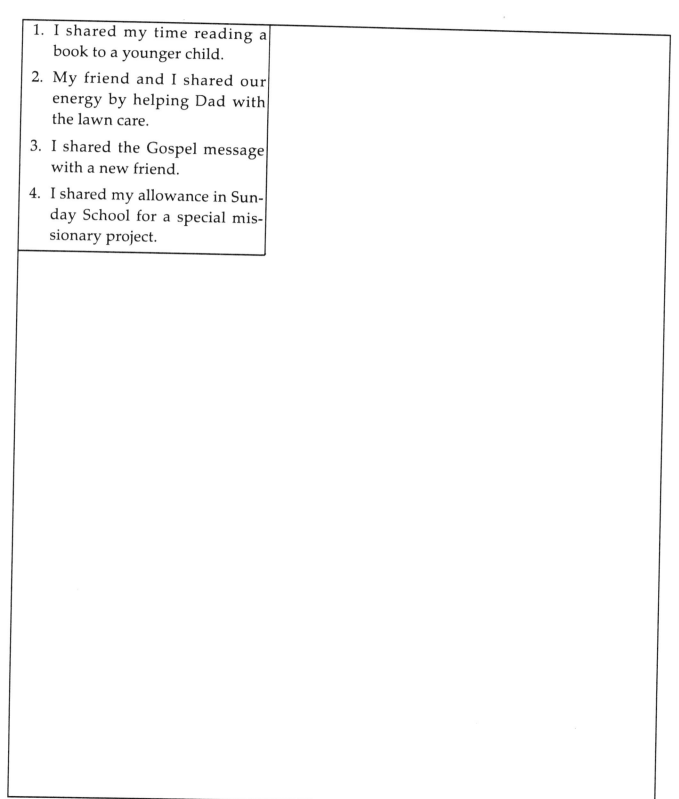

SS2828

Things I Share

"Now he who supplies seed . . . will enlarge the harvest of your righteousness. . . . so that you can be generous on every occasion. . . ."

2 Corinthians 9:10-11

Color the pictures of the things you could share with other people.

SS2828

God Shares with Me

Follow the dotted line from each hand shape to the matching blank. On the blank, write the letter that is in the hand shape.

"... God so loved ...

that he _ _ _ _

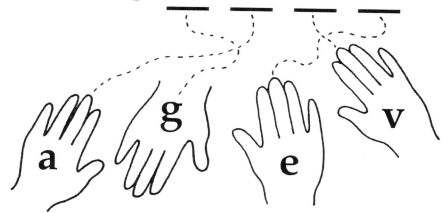

his one and only

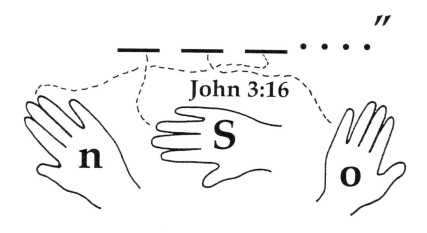

John 3:16

_ _ _ _ ...."

Sharing Makes Me Happy!

"If ye know these things, happy are ye if ye do them."   John 13:17 (KJV)

Fill in the face to show how you look when you share with others. If you wish, you can color the eyes and add hair to your picture.

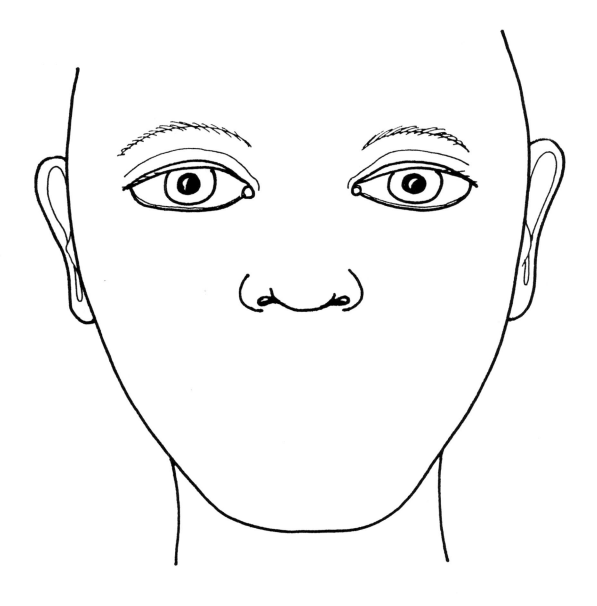

Growing Things

According to the Scripture verse references written on the plants below, Christians are to grow or abound in certain things. Following the arrow around the flower petals, write down each letter to make a word. The words will be things we should grow in.

Growing in Christ

Color the pictures of the things you do to grow in your Christian life.

SS2828

Bible Addition

2 Peter 1:5-7 are "adding" verses. They tell you what important things to add to your faith in Christ. Find out what these things are by filling in the missing letters for the words below. Use the secret code to find the answers.

Secret Code:

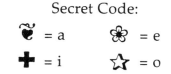

♥ = a   ❀ = e

✚ = i   ☆ = o

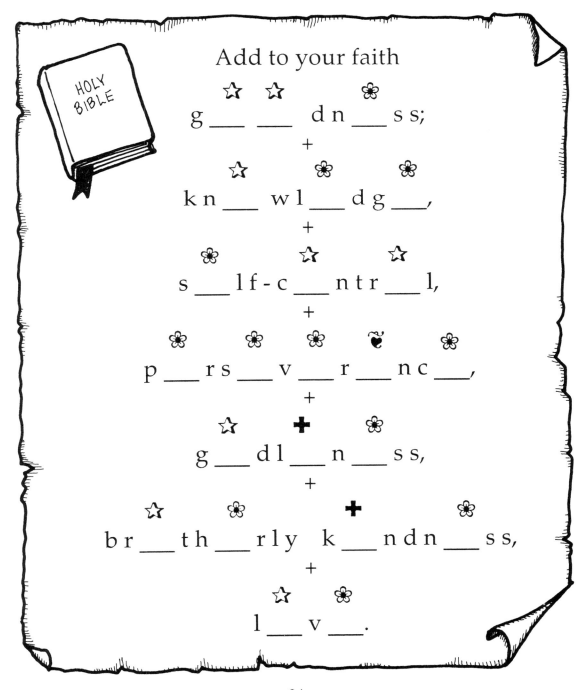

Add to your faith

g ☆__ ☆__ d n ❀__ s s;

+

k n ☆__ w l ❀__ d g ❀__,

+

s ❀__ l f - c ☆__ n t r ☆__ l,

+

p ❀__ r s ❀__ v ❀__ r ♥__ n c ❀__,

+

g ☆__ d l ✚__ n ❀__ s s,

+

b r ☆__ t h ❀__ r l y k ✚__ n d n ❀__ s s,

+

l ☆__ v ❀__.

Thanks Giving Message

"For everything God created is good, and nothing is to be rejected if it is received with thanksgiving. . . ."   1 Timothy 4:4

List things you want to thank God for; use each letter of the words below as the first letter of a word in your list. To help you, several ideas have already been given.

T _____

H _____

A _____

N _____

K ind friends _____

Y ummy food _____

O _____

U nselfish mother _____

G _____

O _____

D _____

Thankful Hearts

Draw a heart shape beside the name of each Bible person who showed a heart of thankfulness for what God did for him/her. Cross out (X) the name of any Bible person who did not have a thankful heart. If you need help, use your Bible to look up the stories about these people.

Hannah
(1 Samuel 1:27-28)

Joseph
(Genesis 45:4-5; 50:20-21)

Cain
(Genesis 4:5-9)

Noah
(Genesis 8:18-21)

King Ahab
(1 Kings 21:1-4)

Blind Bartimaeus
(Mark 10:51-52)

Jonah
(Jonah 4:7-9)

Naaman
(2 Kings 5:13-15)

One of the Ten Lepers
(Luke 17:11-16)

Mary
(Luke 7:37-39, 47)

Job's Wife
(Job 2:9)

My Thankfulness

Poster

HOLY BIBLE

I am thankful for this special verse:
(Write out the Scripture verse or phrase.)

_____

_____

_____

I am especially grateful for
these people:

_____

_____

_____

Some sentences I can use to show I am thankful:

Thank you for helping me. _____

_____

_____

A Bible person with a thankful attitude:

_____

God has blessed me with many things.

(Draw pictures to show some of the things God has given you.)

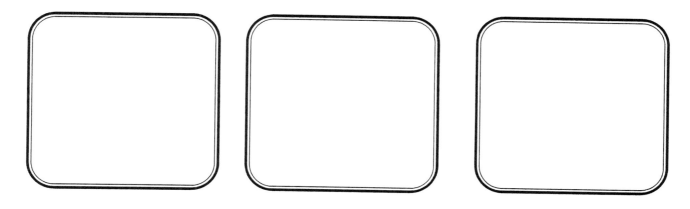

This week I will write a thank-you note to this person:

_____

Here are some prayer requests that God has answered for me:

_____

_____

My prayer list

I'm Thankful

"Let the peace of Christ rule in your hearts, since as members of one body you were called to peace. And be thankful."

Colossians 3:15

Circle the things that you are thankful for. Thank God for them, too!

SS2828

Thank You, Lord

List several items that you are thankful for; then tell a way that you can use each item to serve the Lord.

I Am Thankful for These Items:	Ways I Can Use Them for God:

SS2828

A Thank-You Puzzle

Look at the pictures in the puzzle below. Write down the names of the items to fill in the empty boxes. You can thank God for each thing pictured.

Bible Hero

Color one (or more) of the Bible characters below. Cut out the picture and glue or tape it to a craft stick. Use the puppet to tell a story about your favorite Bible hero.

Animal Scavenger Chase

Locate the following references in your Bible. Read the verse and find the animal(s) that is mentioned. Match the Bible reference with the correct animal picture. Hint: Pictures may be used more than once, and a verse may have more than one animal named in it.

Psalm 20:7   Genesis 8:8

1 Samuel 17:37   Matthew 18:12

Isaiah 11:7

New Things

Think of the word for the picture beneath each blank. Write the first letter of that word in the blank above the picture. You will discover some of the new things mentioned in the Bible.

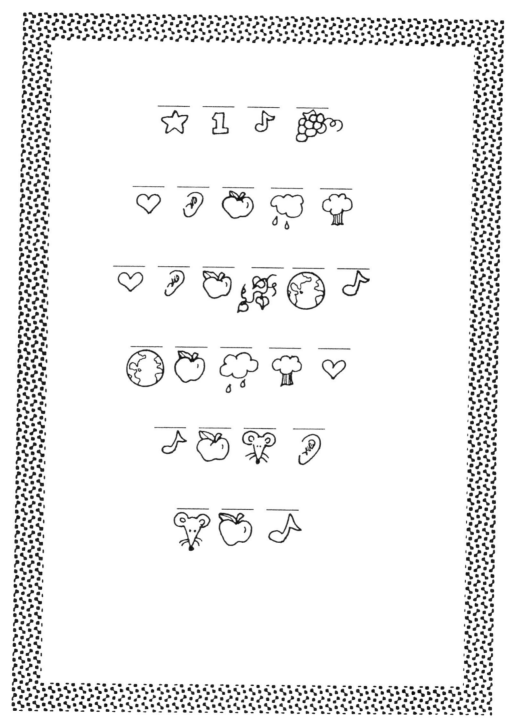

Who's My Mother?

Match the names of the children to their mothers by drawing a line to the matching shape.

Miriam,
Moses,
and
Aaron

Eunice
2 Timothy 1:1-5

Esau
and
Jacob

Rachel
Genesis 30:25; 35:18

Timothy

Jochebed
Numbers 26:59

Joseph
and
Benjamin

Rebekah
Genesis 25:25-26

SS2828

Answer Key

page 6
"A man that hath friends must show himself friendly."

page 8
1. Christ
2. Abraham
3. Daniel
4. Jonathan
5. Naomi
6. Paul

page 10
"I am _a_ fri_e_nd t_o_ _all_ wh_o_ f_ea_r y_ou_, to _all_ wh_o_ f_oll_ow _your_ pre_c_epts."
Psalm 119:63

page 11
What five letters are left? I U E S S
What do these five letters spell? J E S U S

page 19
b_e_d, t_r_ash, d_i_shes, s_in_ks, toys

page 20
Jesus, Others, Yourself

page 22
". . . there will be more rejoicing in heaven over one sinner who repents . . ." Luke 15:7
"When they saw the star, they were overjoyed." Matthew 2:10
"But the fruit of the spirit is love, joy . . . ." Galatians 5:22
". . . and no one will take away your joy." John 16:22
"Restore to me the joy of your salvation. . . ." Psalm 51:12
"Those who sow in tears will reap with songs of joy." Psalm 126:5

page 23
"Who for the joy set before Him endured the cross."
d_i_ed on the _c_ _r_ _o_ _s_ _s_

page 24
Jesus, joy, passing, heart

page 26
Place smiling faces by these words: forgiving, patient, loving, friendly. Place frowning faces by these words: mean, selfish.

page 27
Jonathan, Mary, Rahab, Joseph, Samaritan

page 28
"Be kind and compassionate to one another, forgiving each other, just as in Christ God forgave you." Ephesians 4:32

page 31
unkind, kind, kind, unkind, kind

page 33
way, week, asked, you

page 35

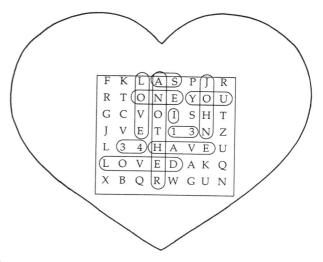

SS2828

page 36
Place smiley faces beside these phrases: Memorizing Bible verses, Attending church, Talking to God in prayer, Reading the Bible, Telling others about God's love, Helping the needy, Singing songs of praise. Place frowning faces beside these phrases: Disobeying parents, Lying to others, Fighting with brothers and sisters, Looking at wicked things, Being selfish.

page 37
received, believed, name, gave, right, children, God

page 39
God Is Love

page 40
The boxed letters are these: e l n e r t a; when I rearrange these, they spell e t e r n a l.

page 44
Teachers, please note the importance of having several "name" books available in your classroom for this activity.

page 45

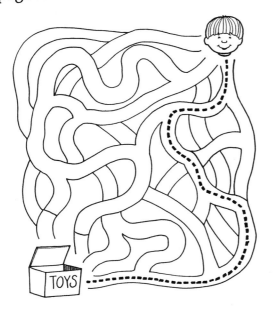

page 48
Circle these pictures: Noah, Abraham, Esther, Christ. Cross out these pictures: Eve, Cain, Israelites, Jonah.

page 49
Hebrews 13:17 = <u>lea</u>d<u>ers</u>
Jeremiah 7:23 = <u>G</u>od
Ephesians 6:1 = <u>paren</u>ts
Joshua 1:7-8 = B<u>oo</u>k of <u>the</u> <u>law</u>

page 56
leave, you, give, not, give, world, not, hearts

page 57
moon-dark sky with stars
man-woman
fruit-tree
fish-water
animals-land

page 59

<u>The</u> <u>power</u> <u>of</u> <u>God</u> <u>for</u> <u>the</u> <u>salvation</u>
  1   2   3   4   5   6   7
<u>of</u> <u>everyone</u> <u>who</u> <u>believes</u>
 8   9   10   11

page 61
Word of God

page 65
These are Bible people who prayed. Circle all the names.

page 66
This is why God wants you to pray to Him for help in changing your ways.

Sin

page 67
Match the following: Daniel with Daniel 6:10, Tax Collector with Luke 18:13, Paul and Silas with Acts 16:25, and Hannah with 1 Samuel 1:10-11.

page 70
Romans 3:23–All have sinned.
Romans 6:23–Wages-death
Romans 6:23–Eternal life
1 John 3:16a–Cross
Romans 10:9–Thank you for dying . . . .
Hebrews 10:17–My sins

page 73

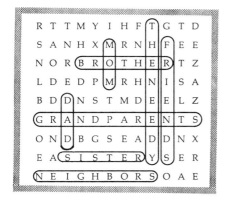

page 78

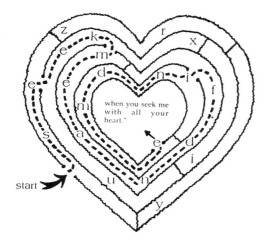

page 79
faith, grace, hope, peace, love

page 81
goodness, knowledge, self-control, perseverance, godliness, brotherly kindness, love

page 83
Heart shapes should be beside these names: Hannah, Joseph, Noah, Blind Bartimaeus, Naaman, One of the Ten Lepers, Mary. These names should be crossed out: Cain, King Ahab, Jonah, Job's Wife.

page 88
rain
toys
family
bike
food

page 90
Psalm 20:7 matched to horse
Genesis 8:8 matched to dove
1 Samuel 17:37 matched to lion and bear
Matthew 18:12 matched to sheep
Isaiah 11:7 matched to cow, bear, and lion

page 91
New things: song, heart, heaven, earth, name, man

page 92
Match Timothy with Eunice; Esau and Jacob with Rebekah; Joseph and Benjamin with Rachel; and Miriam, Moses, and Aaron with Jochebed.

SS2828

Awards

Friendship

_____, thank you for
        name

helping_____

_____.

_____
signature

Kindness

_____, you helped
        name

make the world a kinder place by _____

_____.

_____
signature

Obedience Recognition

_____, I have
        name

noticed_____

_____.

_____
signature

Bible Knowledge Award

Congratulations,

_____, on your good
        name

work in _____.

_____
signature

SS2828